Welcome

Hi kids! I hope you enjoy this Christmas coloring book! First off, I just want to greet you and your family a Merry Christmas and a Happy New Year! Christmas is my favorite holiday!

I have compiled a variety of different Christmas coloring scenes for you to enjoy and will last you for days, even after Christmas is over! The best part is -- it doesn't have to be Christmas for you to color these pages, because the spirit of the holidays should be with us all year long. Since I am a lover of quotes, you will find some pages have the cutest holiday quotes to uplift your mood as well as holiday spirit! I wish you the best always and I hope this book brings you joy and happiness!

Any questions, feel free to visit www.MonaLizaSantos.com and send me a message. Have an amazing day and take care! I wish you and yours the Merriest Christmas and a safe and Happy New Year!

Respectfully,

Mona Liza Santos

Tips: I would suggest coloring with wax crayons or colored pencils rather than markers to avoid the colors going through the next page. But then again, it's your coloring pages - so feel free to do whatever works best for you! Enjoy ♥

Dedicated to my son - Michael Blade, I Love you! To the ones who purchased this coloring book, thank you so much and I am grateful for your support! ♥

- Mona Liza

ISBN: 978-195556-05-35 (Paperback)

First edition

https://www.monalizasantos.com/coloring-books

This Book Belongs To:

_____

_____

_____

COLOR TEST PAGE

BLESSED SEASON

CHRISTMAS IS IN THE AIR

CHRISTMAS ISN'T A SEASON

IT'S A FEELING!

HAVE A MAGICAL AND BLISSFUL CHRISTMAS!

PEACE ON EARTH

DEAR SANTA, I'M TOO CUTE FOR THE NAUGHTY LIST!

PEACE ON EARTH WILL COME TO STAY, WHEN WE LIVE CHRISTMAS EVERY DAY

LET THERE BE PEACE ON EARTH

I'M DREAMING OF A WHITE CHRISTMAS...

SENDING LOTS OF LOVE

YOUR WAY!

JOY, LOVE AND PEACE ALWAYS!

THE TRUE SPIRIT OF CHRISTMAS IS LOVE

GOOD TIDINGS WE BEAR

TO YOU AND YOUR FAMILY!

MERRY AND BRIGHT!

SLEIGH RIDES AND HOT COCOA

THOUGH WE'RE APART, YOU'RE IN MY HEART THIS CHRISTMAS AND ALWAYS

CHRISTMAS IS A TIME FOR FAMILIES

BABY IT'S COLD OUTSIDE

I LOVE SANTA

CHRISTMAS COOKIES AND HAPPY HEARTS, THIS IS HOW THE HOLIDAY STARTS!

BELIEVE IN THE MAGIC
OF CHRISTMAS

CHEERS TO A LOVELY CHRISTMAS SEASON!

HAPPY HOLIDAYS!

How did you like coloring these pages?
Your satisfaction is my priority, so it would be a great
help if you could leave me an honest review on Amazon.

Here are the steps:
1)   Visit Amazon.com
2)   Type in my name Mona Liza Santos in the search on Amazon
3)   Search this coloring book title
4)   Once you find my coloring book, kindly leave me a review

For more updates on my coloring books, please visit:
www.monalizasantos.com/coloring-books

I also write children's books as well, so if your kids love to read,
please check out my site at www.monalizasantos.com
for my latest children's books!

THANK YOU FOR THE LOVE AND SUPPORT!
HAVE AN AMAZING DAY! STAY BLESSED AND FOCUSED ON YOUR DREAMS...

Till Next Time....

And Remember -

Be The Reason Someone Smiles Today!